René Cintré

Fougères

Fougères, medieval city.
Its feudal castle, its belfry, its timber framed houses,
the remnants of its ramparts, its churches and towers stand out in the setting.
Sumptuous buildings, bear witness to a prestigious past, but also weather-beaten ruins,
miraculously preserved from destruction, make way for the town we know today
and which reminds us of relentlessly renewed history,
always at the heart of what was and still remains the border zone
between Brittany, Maine and Normandy.

Photographs: Marc Chauvin
Translation: Andrev Roparz, TREIÑ

ÉDITIONS OUEST-FRANCE
13, rue du Breil, Rennes

At the foot of the castle the rendezvous with history

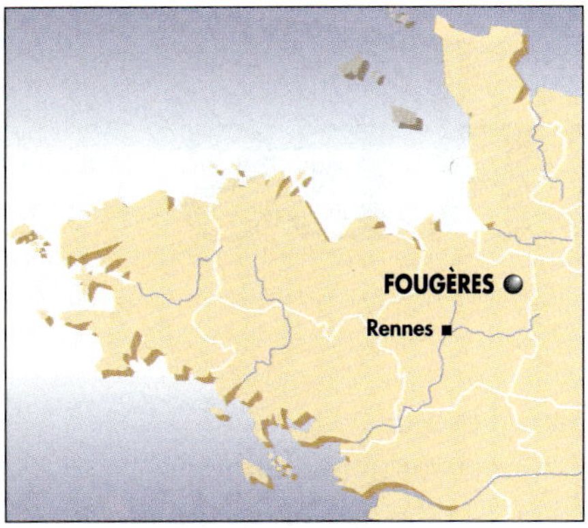

Some places carry the mark of their destiny more than others. Such is the barony of Fougères, born a thousand years ago at the heart of what used to be called, in the Middle-Ages, the Marches of Brittany: really a border zone located on the eastern limits of the Duchy, described from then on by everyone as being in an absolutely unique situation, on the fringes of the great territorial jurisdictions of the times; a land of contacts and exchanges, but also a place of frequent fighting between the neighbouring principalities, and the favourite theatre of events which marked the common history of Brittany and France. And, in the middle of all, a magnificent vessel of stone sailing along the streams of time and swept along many times by the troubles.

In 1166, when Henry II Plantagenet literally took over Brittany in order to include it in the gigantic political entity stretching from England to Aquitaine, via Normandy, Maine, Anjou and Poitou. This is when the anguish of the feudal wars came down on the land: the castle was completely burned down, the town devastated, the inhabitants forced to flee to the forest... but their

Overall view on the south side of town dominated by the belfry.

honour was safe, thanks to Raoul II, the landlord (1150-1194) who refused to accept the situation and was soon promoted to the rank of the greatest defender of the ducal cause !

Then during the years 1220-1230, marked this time by the struggle between the royal power - in the form of Louis IX - and the duke Pierre Mauclerc, who was himself in a very weak position: against the king naturally, but also against the new title holder of Fougères, namely Raoul III (1212-1256), who had sided with the strongest and threatened the border with an unacceptable reversal. This was later followed, in 1225, by the construction of the famous keep of Saint-Aubin du Cormier, built as a challenge to the king by the duke, who was extremely aware of what was really at stake in their power struggle.

Also when Du Guesclin - then Constable of France - took over the town in 1373, in the midst of the hundred years war; it was the starting point of the systematic reconquering of all the other Breton areas left under English occupation.

Again in 1449, during the night of the 24th to the 25th of March, when a kind of unscrupulous adventurer named François de Surienne climbed over the town wall on behalf of the king of England, *committing atrocious crimes, sacrileges, lighting fires and raping women... and other damages too pitiful to tell; all of it by surprise during the sacred time of Lent*! An account of an extremely far-reaching event, to the extent of the emotion it created, and which goes far beyond simple local history. A major event, related by all chroniclers, which eventually led the hundred years war into its terminal phase.

Finally, in July 1488, when the place foundered under the blows of the French army led by La Trémoïlle: a last surrender after those of Châteaubriant, Ancenis and Vitré; a last setback before the final battle of Saint-Aubin-du-Cormier (July 28th), following which Brittany lost its independence.

Fougères seen from the height of the castle.

The medieval city: unveiling the horizon

Many centuries passed of rather eventful history during which nonetheless Fougères never stopped growing and changing. And it is at the end and high point of this evolution - in the 15th century - that it reached its peak, reflecting the image of an active, rich and prosperous town of 4,000 inhabitants, much more so than any of the other towns of the Marches region, with the exception of Vitré which was roughly of the same size. It is also during the last centuries of the Middle Ages, that it took on the aspect of a real garrison town placed as a border outpost.

The fortification effort started very early by the first direct barons was continued without a break by their successors from the houses of Lusignan (1256-1314), France (1314-1328), Alençon (1328-1428)... and the house of Brittany, from 1428; from which date the barony was effectively attached to the ducal domain. During that entire period, the general impression was that of a huge construction site stimulated by a real building frenzy.

Thus the town enclosure was finished for the main part as a major element of its defence, along with the castle, of which there only remains large remnants. Hampered by the constraints of a particularly steep site, this enclosure formed a very cramped setting for the walled town which we can still admire from various view points overlooking the Nançon valley, or better still from the top of the Saint-Leonard steeple which has been especially prepared to cater for visitors: a nostalgic vision of the ancient town-fortress, nestled in the heart of the sleeping country which continues to stand on guard in the form of an invitation to go back into the past for a trip.

A renewed vision of the medieval Fougères beyond the centuries: the town itself and its agglutinated suburbs, a belt of small gardens glued to

For Victor Hugo, the scene was that of "the most beautiful towers in the world: I've seen that under the sun, I've seen it at sundown, I've seen it again in the moonshine and I'm not tired of it; it is wonderful."

the town wall, quarries on the scorched slopes, a few vines here and there and, right at the end of the last pastures towards the east, the forest; the forest which stretched out as far as the eye could see and brought to mind the imminent dangers of the border. Finally, overlooking everything, the belfry: this is the oldest belfry in Brittany, built in 1397, and the only one left along with that of Dinan; a sign of vigilance, certainly, but also of power and success, like the local bourgeoisie, which was from then on in a position to govern itself.

A reassuring vision indeed, because the town attracted, protected and comforted the country people confronted with the misfortunes of the time. During the years 1420-1430, marked by the excesses of total war around the Mont-Saint-Michel, the area was thrown into the harshest of crises: harvests plundered, mills devastated, populations ransomed, fields abandoned, villages deserted; without even mentioning the incredible proliferation of wolves. And, incidental to this drama, the town and castle were considered as a last refuge, so much so that in 1437, *nobody could find a place to stay* !

▷ View of the town wall, on the south side, with the Nicot tower in the foreground.

▽ Fougères: border town, army town and capital of the Marches of Brittany in the Middle Ages.

The urban landscape: images and impressions

Like almost all of the towns of the Middle Ages, Fougères was made up of two well distinguished parts: the walled town, locked within its ramparts and opening onto the outside through four gates, of which only the Porte Notre-Dame, built in 1477, remains today, and the suburbs, located close to the gates, but outside the walls.

First the walled town which, unfortunately as everyone will notice, has lost most of its original character, following numerous reconstructions over the centuries, due themselves to so many irrecoverable losses (wear and tear of time, great fires of the 18th century, depredations of the 19th century, bombardments of June 6th and 9th 1944).

View of the Saint-Sulpice suburb from the public gardens esplanade. In the Middle Ages, it was the artisans' area: "weavers, tanners, blacksmiths... and other trades people".
Archives départementales d'Ille-et-Vilaine 2 A 29.

▽ ***Map of the town in the Middle Ages.***
From a sketch by R. Cintré.

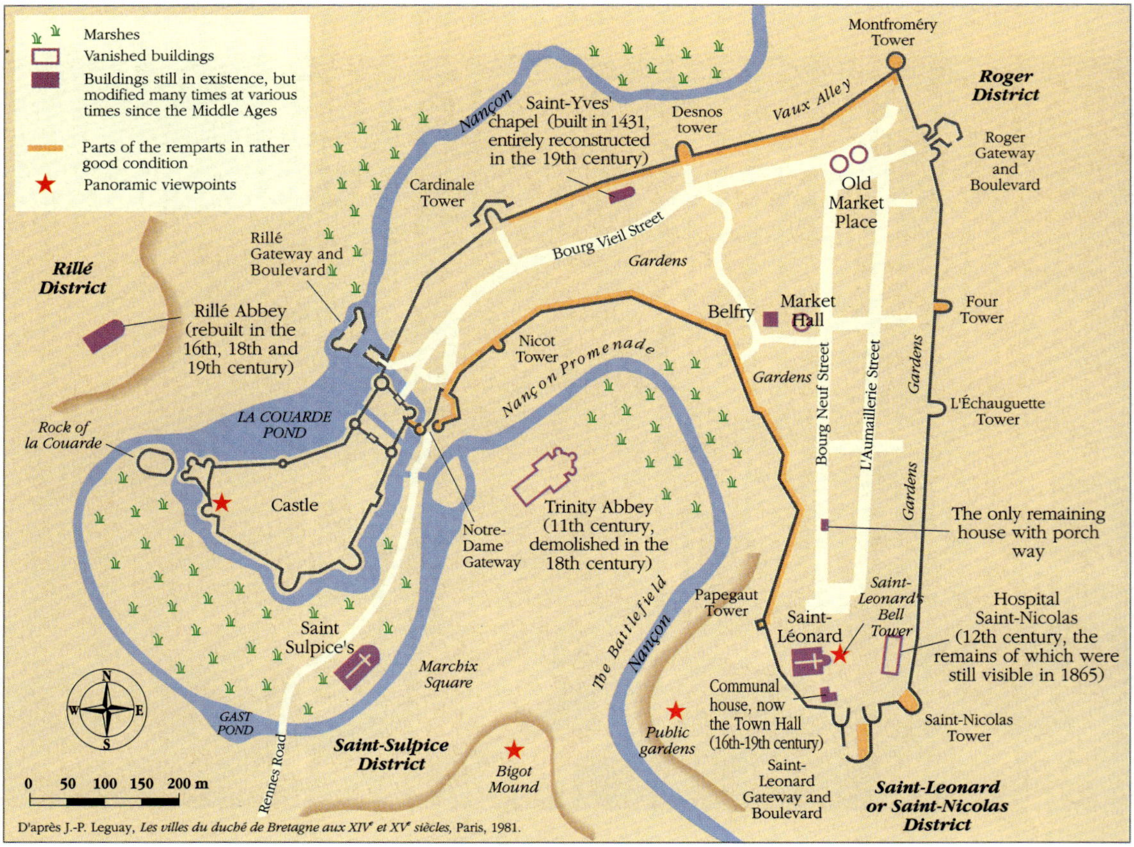

D'après J.-P. Leguay, *Les villes du duché de Bretagne aux XIVe et XVe siècles*, Paris, 1981.

The belfry.

And yet the streets pattern is still the same, along three main axis: rue de la Pinterie - called du Bourgvieil at first - which makes the link between the castle and the upper town; rue Nationale - or du Bourgneuf - leading towards Saint-Léonard's; and rue Chateaubriand - parallel to the latter - formerly called de l'Aumaillerie, because the largest cow market of the area was held here. It is hard, however, to imagine what the urban landscape itself could have been like, made as it was of a series of densely built blocks of houses, porches, shops, religious buildings and even gardens which, according to the old saying, came biting at the thick walls of the said town. So we will pay more attention to the elements which are still alive in this scenery: the ramparts, dressed in 13th, 14th and 15th century fashion; the belfry - superb! - that has previously been mentioned; the town hall, bearing in part the decorative seal of the Renaissance and, of

The belfry

Built in the 14th century, altered in the 16th, it is a very elegant and beautiful octagonal tower crowned by a flamboyant gallery, itself topped by a bell-tower from the 18th century.

The gate of Notre-Dame, built in 1477 on the site of ancient fulling mills which were demolished to do so.

Saint-Léonard's church, "on a beautiful shadowy esplanade, a real belvedere from the top of which one can soar over vast spaces..." (A. Robida)

Saint-Léonard's church

Built towards the end of the 11th century, it was completely rebuilt starting in 1380; the start of a very long sequence of works, the phases of which can still be easily figured out :

- end of 14th - 15th century, construction of the nave: magnificent example of architecture called multiple gables, very much appreciated in the Marches area (like in Vitré, La Guerche or Rannée), and perfectly identifiable along the north and south aisles; flat chevet with large window and no transept.
- 16th century: in all probability, the rebuilding of the exterior face and construction of a Renaissance inspired gallery along the north aisle.
- 17th century: construction of the steeple, finished in 1675.
- 19th century: last great alterations consisting of a complete turning around of the building in order to put the door where the choir was located (1860-1880). Consequently, a new high altar was built in 1873 in the purest neogothic style of the period and, above all, a new facade, also in a neogothic style, which is still unfortunately lacking the patina of time.

course, Saint-Leonard's church, one of the finest examples of Gothic art in the region, casting its magnificent, easily recognisable outline, on the horizon.

As for the suburbs, only Saint-Sulpice - also called faubourg du gast, in memory of its marshy origins - still reflects the vision of the Middle Ages. The sensation of a world apart, tightly snuggled against the castle, which brings us back at the heart of the medieval hive; a world full of artisans working to the rhythm of the perpetual motion of a dozen mills... grist mills, fulling mills, tanning mills, and

Saint-Léonard: view of the neogothic facade (19th century) and the bell-tower (15th-17th century).

△ *Saint-Sulpice: view of the choir and the high altar, magnificently restored in all their brightness (18th century).*

▷ *Saint-Sulpice's church, which must be visited throughout to see the various stages of its construction (15th-18th century).*

▽ *Gargoyle from Saint-Sulpice's church.*

Saint-Sulpice's church

Started in the 14th century, it shows all the signs of a long term construction, so much so that the nave was not finished before 1540, at which time the building of the choir began... which lasted until the 18th century! As for the steeple, it went up between 1460 and 1490. And the whole makes a very beautiful late gothic ensemble, kept homogeneous nonetheless through the exclusive use of granite, as well as the perfect integration of the elements of decoration made of kale motifs, decorated pinnacles, monstrous gargoyles and also rather naughty figures spread out all around the building.

Inside the church, a whole series of little side chapels shows the evolution of the building. Among those we will mention on the south side the chapel called des Tanneurs (mid 16th century), which offers the vision of a superb granite retable, finely chiselled along the theme of the instruments of the Passion of Christ. And, on the north side, the Notre-Dame chapel (consecrated in 1502): generously decorated, it houses the famous statue of the Lady of the Marshes. Otherwise, the eye is easily caught by the magnificence of the 18th century furniture: a perfect illustration of the rocaille style made of wainscoted panels, assorted marbles, bright sculptures (made by Antoine Violard), gilded woodwork... and a thousand other glitters.

also, at the end of the era, paper mills.

As a matter of fact, life in this area was regulated by four main activities. First of all drapery, certainly very old and, in any case, attested in the 14th century: Fougières-la-rons where they made drapes, according to the chronicler... But it developed mainly after 1420, with the arrival of numerous Norman refugees - expert in the art of drapery - who were driven from their homes by the hardships of war. Then dyeing, favoured by the quality of the water of the river Nançon. Together, they contributed to the international fame of the scarlet fabrics of Fougères.

Also tanning, established here as early as the 12th century, which brought the development of all forms of leather and skin processing: sheep, calf, rabbit, fox, wolf, marten, weasel, otter - which abounded in our rivers in those days - wild cat, and even dogskin, which were of an incomparable quality for making gloves.

Purse-making, glove-making, baldric-making, parchment-making, fur-

Monsters coming out of the wall, guardians of the place and the time, these are the other gargoyles from Saint-Sulpice's church.

dressing... the list would be too long of all the uses that could stem from that industry, most of them geared to the local trade. And finally pintery, which is the making of pewter objects, the memory of which has been kept in the name of one of the main streets of our town.

All of these activities took place around the castle and the church. The church above all, full of symbols for the parishioners who had built it with their own hands, on the very site were

View of the four mills, also called the La Tranchée mills.

- according to the tradition - the statue of the Lady of the marshes was found; lost since 1166, it was the object of an intense devotion due to its miraculous powers, *with the grace of Our Lord... and the alms of the good catholic people*! On the other hand, there is nothing left of another building, the traces of which are only to be found in the archives. It is the priory of the Trinity, dated from the 11th century: a splendid roman edifice inspired from the Touraine area, over 50 metres long, which was completely destroyed in 1786 because it was threatening to collapse. It is a pity, really, because it seems that it was one of the finest abbeys in all of Brittany.

Finally, it is impossible to complete this first glance at the town without mentioning the commercial importance of this town as cross-roads, one of the main entrances and exits of the duchy. Everything was to be found there: foods of all kinds and from all sources; animals of all kinds imported from the neighbouring provinces; wool from Spain, drapes from Flanders, England and Normandy, canvas from Brittany and many other goods both locally produced and from the international trade, or even from far away countries like Ireland, Scotland, Italy and others. And, still remaining at the same place, the *place du Marchix*, carrying from generation to generation the memories of the fairs of Fougères, including the famous Angevines made in 1506, which still continue today to mark the passing of time. A sensation of the eternal round of time, through the unchanging return of the seasons, the days and the hours...

The castle, a lord among the stones

The castle of Fougères, main piece of the Breton defence network, is without contest the most important citadel of the Marches region, both in terms of its size and the quality of its remains, and in terms of the role it always played at the junction of the events which governed the great destinies of the ducal state. From its shapes and the impression it gives, it also remains the best example of the continuous evolution of medieval military architecture which lasted for five centuries, from the 11th to the 15th century, in parallel to the no less continuous evolution of the war techniques. Consequently, new elements were continuously added, each corresponding to a new period and all perfectly integrated around the four main functions: the Advanced Works (12th-13th century), the great castle enclosure, enclosing an area of more than 2 hectares; the Recess, which played the role of ultimate hideout inside the place; and the Postern (15th century).

From then on, one needs a lot of scope and plenty of imagination to reinsert the whole castle in its original location: a huge rock emerging from a

View of the Advanced Works from the outside with the La-Haye-Saint-Hilaire tower in the middle.

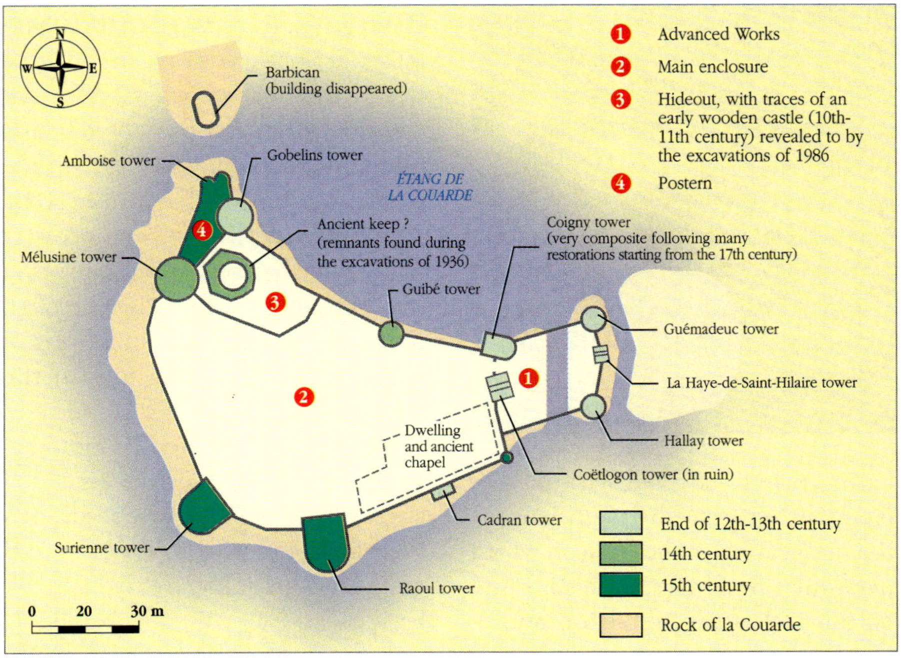

The various periods of construction of the castle. From a sketch by R. Cintré.

View of the inside of the Advanced Works with, from left to right: the Guémadeuc tower, the La-Haye-de-Saint-Hilaire tower and the Halley tower (late 12th - 13th century).

◁ *Levelled remains of an old stone keep about which almost nothing is known (13th-14th century?), also showing the top of the rock where the castle was originally located.*

▷ *View of the south curtain of the Advanced Works, to which are also linked the town's ramparts, starting with the gate of Notre Dame, with the Plesguen tower on the right. In the middle, the Halley tower with the water system at its foot: this system was equipped with a rather advanced mechanism for the time in order to flood the Advanced Works in the event of an attack on this side.*

basin entirely covered with marshland, cut off from the main land by the meandering of the Nançon which plays the role of natural moats. And on this rock, from the 11th century - perhaps even the 10th century -, a wooden construction was erected, of which nothing is left, except the traces discovered on the ground during the excavations of 1986. Burnt down completely in 1166 by Henry II Plantagenet, this first generation building was immediately replaced by the stone castle that we know, which was constructed progressively by Raoul II from the year 1170, starting with the structures called l'Avancée (the Advanced Works). On the other hand, there has been much talk about the supposed previous existence of an old stone keep, the foundations of which were found in 1936 in the middle of the Réduit. In fact, we know almost nothing about this building, with a circular shape on the inside and a polygonal design on the outside, neither its date, nor its role, nor even if more than its foundations had ever been built!

Inside the castle, view of the Coètlogon (12th c.) and Coigny (13th-17th c.) towers. Facing the Halley tower, its architectural counterpart, the Coètlogon tower is totally in ruins today, having been dismantled in the 19th century.

The Advanced Works (l'Avancée) (late 12th-13th century)

As such, it is the first series of ingenious fortifications, constructed in order to defend the entrance to the castle and has all the signs of 13th century military architecture: persistent square shapes, loopholes built in the most classical way possible (some were transformed into gun holes during the 15th century), a single door, vaulted and protected by a double portcullis and a ditch. There is no trace of a drawbridge, but only of a removable footbridge, easy to remove in case of danger (it was replaced by a fixed stone bridge in the 18th century).

View of the so-called Gobelins tower, which is another name for imps or elves!

The Gobelins tower

A slightly flattened cone shape, it dates back to the late 12th or early 13th century; a true keep constructed on one the best defended points of the place (27 metres high, 4 stories and a basement separated by floors; 3.5 metres thick at the base).

Inside the main enclosure, the ruins of the lord's lodging and the castle chapel, completely demolished between 1810 and 1820 in order to reclaim the stone!

View of the small Guibé tower, shaped as a corbelled pepper-pot sitting on the great north curtain (15th century).

View of the Mélusine tower (14th) camped on its rock, onto which the Postern curtain is grafted (15th c.).

Double following page: Fougères today: image of a bygone era... and of history eternally recommencing.

The Mélusine tower

It takes its name from the fairy Mélusine, who was as everyone knows the protective fairy of the Lusignans, who became Lords of Fougères in 1256. Mélusine, as a maternal, land-clearing and building fairy, is also the incarnation of the myth of the woman-serpent, a symbol - highly significant - of the versatility of time and fortune. And this is how the construction around the year 1300 of the most beautiful tower of the castle was placed under her patronage: over 30 metres high, 13 metres diameter, with walls 3.60 metres thick, stemming from a remarkable talus-shaped base straight off the rock. Inside, there are four floored stories, linked by a magnificent spiral staircase, comfortable rooms for the times: lit, heated... and primitive toilets close to the watch stations. Underground, there is a cellar shaped as a dungeon to keep the food fresh... and, perhaps, to throw in some poor fellows sentenced to a somewhat uncomfortable stay in those badly renowned *oubliettes*.

Mélusine tower, Gobelins tower and, in the foreground, a view of the great south-south-west curtain, with its very beautiful row of crenels, merlons and machicolations.

The Raoul and Surienne towers

They bear witness to the importance of the works carried out during the 1480's by Duke François II in order to improve the fortification of the place. In fact, the great south-western curtain was due to be reinforced, as it appeared really very weak with the potential use of canons as a more

View of the Amboise tower, also called the Postern, where the drawbridge grooves can still be seen (15th century).

The postern

Added after 1449, the Postern grafted onto the western end of the main enclosure and consists of many different elements: two curtains, one leading from the Mélusine tower, the other from the Gobelins tower. Then the Amboise tower - as a homage to Françoise d'Amboise, wife of the duke Pierre II, baron of Fougères from 1442 to 1456 - , was formed by two corbelled semi turrets resting on a solidly built up base. The actual door, which nowadays opens right onto the cliff, was originally linked to another loophole shaped building occupying the rest of the rock.

View of the Raoul and Surienne towers, certainly among the most beautiful artillery towers of the end of the Middle Ages existing in Brittany.

and more efficient instrument of attack.

The Raoul and Surienne towers were added, examples of a truly marvellous adaptation of the structures to the unprecedented progress of the powder artillery: a horseshoe type of construction, like the ones in Nantes, Dinan or Clisson; walls 7 metres thick at the base, which is quite unheard of, not less than 20 metres diameter with a projection of about 15 metres from the rampart; five stories topped by a large specially designed platform; numerous blockhouses built into the walls. All of it, however, was built for nothing because - as was already mentioned previously - the place fell almost without opposition on July 9th 1488, under the pounding of the French attack which were overwhelming in their numbers, quality and determination to win.

Close-up on the machicolations, decorated with trefoil motifs, mostly characteristic of the constructions carried out during the reign of François II, Duke of Brittany and Baron of Fougères from 1458 to 1488.

The great sleep (1532-1789)

Everyone knows what happened after the battle of Saint-Aubin-du-Cormier: first of all the wedding of Duchess Anne of Brittany to King Charles VIII of France († 1498), then to his heir Louis XII († 1515), which led eventually to the signing of the Union Act of 1532 sealing the final union of Brittany to the kingdom of France. From then on, the role of the border was bound to become more blurred, and our town *did not delay in becoming a bourgeois and peaceful town, after having been a noble and warring citadel.* An account of a kind of sleepiness, which is also noticeable through the appearance of the town which remained unchanged until the end of the 17th century in its purest form inherited from the Middle Ages. With a slightly higher population, of course, of about 6,000 in 1782, made almost entirely however of artisans of a comparatively lowly status. Working practices change with the times... Now the manufacturing and trading of cloth is the main activity: heavy linen and canvas cloth, of a rather crude quality - albeit strictly checked through a compulsory marking system - geared to appropriate outlets and shipped mainly through the ports of Nantes and Saint-Malo. All in all, it was enough to supply a rather fluctuating production of between 6,000 and

Fougères in 1610, a water-colour copy of a print by Claude Chastillon, the king's topographer, on which one can recognise all the constituent elements of a medieval landscape.

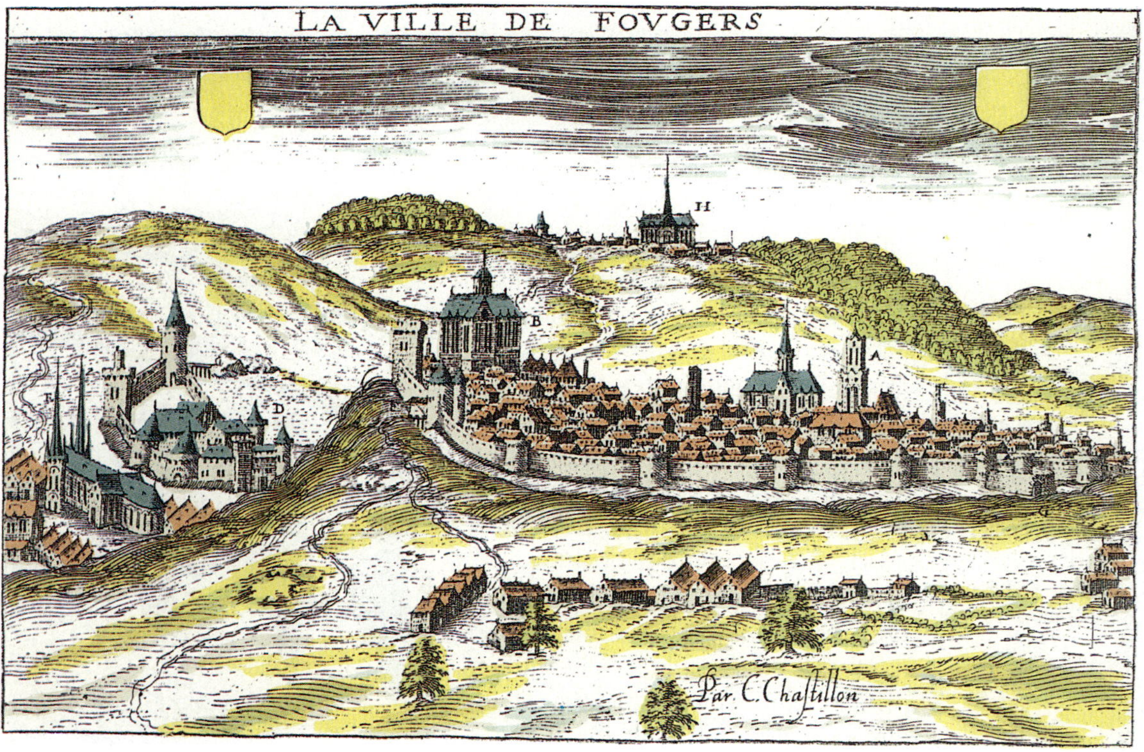

12,000 items per year at the end of the 18th century, when the ups and downs of the situation were already setting the framework for a coming decline.

In the meantime, Fougères - still considered as a necessary transit and warehousing town - remained for a long time one of the largest centres in the country for trading cereals, cattle and salt. Salt above all, because its value could easily be increased ten, fifteen or twenty times in Normandy and in Maine due to the royal gabelle (salt tax), which made the area a preferred place for a throng of elusive smugglers: strange nightly trips, the history of which was known only by the wind, through the forest and along the tracks of Gâtesel and the fords of the border rivers. These fleeting images of the residual character of the border remained until the end of the Kingdom of France... along with the great fiscal injustice which opposed Brittany to the rest of the Kingdom!

The Raoul tower.

Despite the continuous passing of time, many significant events have nonetheless contributed to change the order of things, from the years 1610-1620, starting with the establishment of new religious congregations in town.

The Urbanistes convent, characteristic of a classical construction of the 17th century: pure lines and forms adorned only with the presence of granite dormer pediments, alternately triangular and round in shape.

Apart from the input of new blood, particularly in the fields of education and hospital care, came the construction of new buildings specifically reflecting the style of the 17th century: 1607, the Recollets (right at the end of rue de la Forêt); the same year, the collège des Ursulines (in the present rue Lesueur); 1633, the arrival of the Clarisses sisters who gave us the magnificent Urbanistes convent (finished in 1689, transformed into a barracks in the 19th century, saved at the last minute from demolition in the 1970s); 1672, the Augustines, affiliated to Saint-Nicolas hospital; 1678, the Saint-Louis general hospital (completely disappeared since).

Then there were the great fires. Indeed, Fougères - like many other cities of the same period - had the sad privilege of being burnt down many times in the course of the 18th century: in 1710, 1734, 1751, 1762, 1788. It was mainly the upper areas of the city which had to suffer from these fires, around the present place du Théâtre. Entire sections of rue Porte-Roger, Nationale and Pinterie were destroyed. The reconstruction which followed immediately launched a new urban design, more modern, more open, and also more official: new alignments, new materials (stone and slate), new facades inspired from the new plans of the period, such as the famous Gabriel plan which was followed for the reconstruction of the Grand-Rue (rue Nationale) and which can be found also in Rennes, another great burnt down city. Almost all the old porch way houses still in existence were destroyed at the same time.

Finally, we recall that it is at the end of the 18th century that the huge and systematic demolition work started on the ramparts... in order to gain some room: the Saint-Léonard gate was pulled down starting in 1773; followed by the Roger and Rillé gates. And the ditches were abandoned, filled or sold to private individuals, turning the pages of history, before the revolution.

Front elevation of the houses of the Grand'Rue (now called rue Nationale) according to the famous Gabriel plan.
Archives départementales d'Ille-et-Vilaine C 388.

The wind of the Revolution

Nowhere escaped the revolution. Here, however, one must recognise that the clash of the opposition forces was particularly brutal and heavily significant, to the point that Balzac and Victor Hugo could both find inspiration in it. More than just romances, *Les Chouans* and *Quatre-vingt-treize* also invite one to reflect on the profound meaning of history:

The castle, viewed at night.

the strength of ideas, the worth of men, the memory of places, the remembrance nourished everywhere of this great renting asunder :

1791-1792 was undoubtedly the major turning point of this period, marked by a sudden worsening of events: the civil constitution of the clergy, the King's flight, the war outside, the nation in danger, Valmy, the Republic; and also, from the beginning, the continuation of the aristocratic plot.

This is when La Rouërie appeared, running from castle to castle, gathering together all the nobles of the area, expending a great deal of energy, who became as of December 1791 the real leader of the Association Bretonne, which was to be the main instrument of the counter-revolution in progress in Brittany.

Stratagem of the republican soldiers, "disguised as counter-Chouans", leaving Fougères through the gate of Notre-Dame... "and whose cheerfulness was more foreboding of a hunting party than a dangerous expedition. For them, the encounters of the Chouannerie, where the Bretons from the towns were fighting against the Bretons from the country, seemed to have replaced the tournaments of the chivalry." Honoré de Balzac.
Print signed Le Blant, illustrating a scene from *Les Chouans* by Balzac, Paris, 1930. Coll. Bibliothèque municipale de Fougères.

The insignia of Vendée shaped as a Sacred-Heart, also worn by the Chouans.
Musées départementaux de Loire-Atlantique, Musée Dobrée, Nantes. Photo Ch. Hémon.

◁◁ ***Fighting near Fougères, reflecting the war of ambushes fought by the Chouans, who were able to assemble spontaneously by the dozen and to disappear just as rapidly, elusive as they were, into the countryside.***
Wood engraving made in 1889 by Le Blant for *Les Chouans,* by Balzac. Bibliothèque municipale de Fougères.

La Rouërie, also recognised by everyone as being perhaps the last great defender of the ancient Breton liberty... albeit - and it has to be said - in the name of no less ancient privileges inherited from the Ancien Régime: a manifestation of one of the most original forms of the counter-revolutionary movement, doomed to disappear with the death of its leader, on January 30th 1793. Finally La Rouërie, whose memory has been constantly honoured by the town of Fougères as one of its most illustrious children.

Spring 1793 - spring 1794, some argue that it is around Landéan, on Saint-Joseph's day (March 19th 1793) that the Chouannerie started, as yet another aspect of the counter-revolution, this time a popular one: rejection of the levy en masse, defence of the King and the good priests, an impression among the peasants that they had been taken in, fear of the future for a number of artisans ruined by a rapid decline of the cloth market, the revolt was certainly much more complex than it seems at first glance, setting up the two Frances, the new and the old, one against the other, in a horrifying civil war which was also echoed in the Vendée. In November 1793, the drama reached its climax when the Vendéens came to

LIBERTÉ, ÉGALITÉ, FRATERNITÉ.

GUERRE AUX CHOUANS,

PAIX AUX CULTIVATEURS RÉPUBLICAINS.

Instructions aux Citoyens officiers municipaux et commandans des détachemens et gardes nationales de l'arrondissement, du Républicain HUMBERT, *général de brigade.*

Extract from a republican propaganda poster for the attention of the people charged with "pacifying the area and delivering it from the wickedness of the Chouans", 1794.
Archives municipales de Fougères.

◁ ***Statue of la Rouërie made by Jean Fréour in 1993 and placed in front of the house where he was born, on April 13th 1751: a hero for Fougères, a Breton of course, but also - and before that - a hero of the American War of Independence (1777-1783) to which he participated with La Fayette under the name colonel Armand.***

Fougères and made an alliance with the Chouans.

This was followed by many weeks of horrible setting of accounts and reciprocal violence, fuelled as well by the re-institution of the Terror until the Spring of 1794: the guillotine installed in the middle of town, dozens of executions, the forest and the countryside thoroughly combed. It is in this context that the figure of Aimé Picquet du Boisguy suddenly appeared, a young squire from Parigné hardly aged 17 at the time, who became general of the Chouans in 1796... and kept the fighting going until the beginning of the 1800s, just as much out of bravado as for the honour of a long lost cause, because it was looking back towards the past. The various events may be listed along with the memory of the places hidden on the edge of sunken lanes, lonely farms, copses and solitary moors: La Croix de recouvrance[1], La Pèlerine[2], Malagra[3], Marigny[4], La Plochais[5]... and so many others, which nowadays have all returned to silence for ever.

Ravages committed by the Chouans in the Fougères area in 1794

"You are no doubt aware of the horrors committed by the Chouans on the 26th of this month on the communes of Mellé and Monthault, taking peaceful young people by force in order to turn them into accomplices of their infamy, they slaughtered five or six individuals; the arrest they made the next day on the road to Fougères, between Landéan and Louvigné, of two cart drivers carrying coffee and other expensive goods, where after having removed all that interested them, they tore into the trunks and boxes which contained them, and spilled the rest on the road... Also we warn you that many of them are marching in groups through the communes, stealing peaceful young people from their work and their families, and getting weapons; and creating alarm and desolation wherever they go. Many young people from our commune have been abducted by force, others have received orders to surrender by a set date or loose their lives. Our undermanned billets are carefully intervening wherever there is danger, but always too late, none of the inhabitants of the land, scared as they are, dare tell us which way they went. So we ask you, citizens, to take the swiftest action in order to save the land from the calamities which afflict it." (Letter from the municipal officers of the commune of Louvigné to the administrative citizens of the district of Fougères, 29th prairial year III, ADIV L467.)

1. Near Landéan, in memory of the Saint-Joseph's day revolt.
2. Between Fougères and Ernée, where Lescure died on November 3rd 1793.
3. In La Bazouge-du-Désert, where Talmont was arrested on December 30th of the same year 1793 before being executed in Laval.
4. In Saint-Germain-en-Coglès, where so many secret meetings were held...
5. Between Fougères and Louvigné, where Boisguy set up his most murderous ambush against the Blues, on July 25th 1795.

Then came the shoe (1850-1975)

After the Revolution, people resumed their normal life, although in a suddenly older setting, reflecting the image of a town between two epochs, surrounded by the halo of the romantic vision at which almost all of the famous writers of the period gazed: Chateaubriand (visiting his sisters), Balzac (looking for characters), Victor Hugo (in the footsteps of Juliette Drouet), Flaubert and Maxime du Camp, Mérimée... without forgetting Albert Robida who used all his talent to describe the vividness of the place: the castle, all garlanded with ivy; the old houses, crammed in a complete jumble; the roof line which seems to be playing off the ground tag... and the ramparts, mutilated, broken, cut, notched and re-notched, repaired here with rubble stone patches, there with holes cut into it, windows and doors; tower trimmings, posterns transformed into garden gates, and loopholes with flower pots. Something like an old iron suit of armour arranged like a dressing gown !

Yet it is in this setting that, around 1850, the shoe industry appeared, a manifestation of a tremendous economic revival derived directly from slipper manufacturing, which had been well established here since the beginning of the 19th century, particularly in the prisons! The idea of replacing felt by leather, and adapting the manufacturing technique, gave birth to the shoe industry.

Fougères in 1810, and already the romantic vision of the medieval ruins. Notice the existence - still at the same period - of the remnants of an old multi-arched bridge in front of the castle postern.
Water coloured print by Bachelot de la Pylaie.

Letterhead from the Cordier enterprises in 1906, located at that time at place Lariboisière, completely demolished during the bombardment of 1944.
Archives municipales de Fougères.

The new activity developed at an extraordinary speed, leading to a literal explosion of the city's population: the number of inhabitants doubled in less than 30 years to reach 21 000 in 1900; there were no less than 12 000 workers at that time, working in forty different factories which soon became one hundred during the 1920s, making Fougères the main working class town in Brittany and the principal town in France for shoe manufacturing: new houses, new buildings (theatre, college, railway station), new areas (like Bonabry where the church was officially opened in 1893), a new spirit, a new bourgeoisie and also a new working class, confronted with the first experiences of the new social struggle.

Nobody better than Jean Guéhenno - this other local son, born in Fougères in 1890, a worker's son

Rue de la Pinterie in the 19th century, by Albert Robida, with its old porch way houses, somewhat shaky, and now totally disappeared since the bombardment of 1944.
In A. Robida, *La vieille France, Bretagne*, Paris, 1892.

△ ***Lock-out in Fougères, November 1906-February 1907.***

◁ ***Inside a factory: the machinists workshop: "the length of the stitches was measured with a roller and we were paid on that basis. But the managers did not count some of the stitches. We had to fight for a centime".***

Extract from *Marie, ou la vie d'une piqueuse, in Le Pays de Fougères*, n° 25, B. Heudré.

who went to a teacher training college, became a teacher, a writer and a member of the French Academy - expressed this glaring aspiration to hold their heads high, driven by the secret hope of changing their lives: it was a matter of bread, of course, but just as much a matter of honour, a hard struggle; the struggle for their recognition and their human dignity, far beyond simple claims for a few pennies. Along this line, the long

Workers solidarity in Fougères (November 1906)

"On the 16th of November, in the premises of the labour exchange, communist soup kitchens are organised. 22 huge stoves provide already 1500 soups. On the morning of the 27th, we can testify that all of the working teams are there. Men and women try to outdo each other in energy and drive. Some are going into the forest to collect dead wood, others travel up and down the streets of the town to collect donations, because the whole population is behind the strikers, shocked as they are by the selfishness of the owners. The women workers light the fire, cut the chunks of beef, prepare the vegetables, melt the fat, draw the cider and work without relent. The scene is impressive... A new live is emerging for this valiant Breton population whose patience is being stretched, but we can sometimes spot in their eyes something like a streak of revolt..." (Extract from an article entitled "The lock-out of Fougères", published in the Thursday 29th of November 1906 issue of *L'Humanité*, ADIV 60 Ma 4.)

Starting in the years 1920-1930, Fougères cultivated its tourist vocation, well located as it is between Vitré and the Mont-Saint-Michel, Combourg, Cancale and Saint-Malo, thanks particularly to the train, which has since ceased to exist however.

strike of 1906-1907 is certainly to be ranked among the most exemplary actions of the beginning of the century, hailed by Jaurès himself who came to the town and often cited in history books as a highly significant reference.

On the contrary, the strike of 1932 was a failure, to be analysed in the context of these grey years, marked by the horrifying recession which affected particularly the pelt and leather industry. After the war came the recovery. There was even a flare-up of economic resurgence during the fifties and sixties, but it did not last long, slashed irrevocably by the very serious crisis of the early seventies, when the factories closed for good one after the other. Today there remains only five or six of them, employing about seven hundred workers, still guaranteeing their remarkable know-how for some of the most prestigious French names in women shoes. On the other hand, however, it must be said that the time of the single industry is well and truly over in Fougères!

Fougères today... and tomorrow

With the population stabilised at around 23,000 inhabitants, Fougères is really a medium size town. Medium size all right, but its importance is amplified by the presence of the country which gravitates around it, with its 85,000 dependants, its potential resources (in the middle of one the most beautiful granite basins in the West of France, as well as the principal cattle-breeding area in France) and its future prospects, at the junction of three provinces soon to be connected to the trans-European communication network. Therein lies Fougères great chance, apart from its ability to overcome hardship, to adapt, to evolve and to transform itself. Over 80% having been destroyed during the terrible bombardments of 1944, the town was rebuilt, not without difficulties of course - this reconstruction lasted until the early sixties - but above all the real concern was rethinking its structure. This is how the boulevard Leclerc was created - it was finished in 1959 - to become rightly or wrongly the main thoroughfare of a new completely redesigned urban centre. Shattered again after the terrible downfall of the shoe industry after 1975, Fougères has been able to react: high-tech industries, electronics, robotics, optical equipment, glass processing, precision mechanics, granite, food-pro-

▽◁ View of the Surienne tower, with its gun holes, widening towards the outside in the modern style.

▽ View of the last remaining porch way house, n° 51 rue Nationale, now housing the museum devoted to Emmanuel de La Villéon.

cessing and a large inter-regional cattle market, these are some of the new activities which bear witness to the ground already covered, while waiting to achieve even more.

In the meantime, Fougères is also cultivating its label of Art and History Town of which it is rightly proud: an exceptional heritage, truly able to appeal to the hundred thousand visitors to the castle each year; its library with particularly rich collections; its archives, opened to the public; its museum devoted to the painter Emmanuel de La Villéon (1858-1944), one of the last known representatives of the impressionist style of painting; its crystal factory, perpetuating the art of blown glass, very rare in France; its wall covered with a trompe-l'oeil painting, not to be missed; its cultural events on the theme of the Living Book, and its very promising Regional Voices festival. All this to tell you that Fougères is continuing its trip, as a magnificent vessel sailing on the wings of time, still well anchored in the heart of what was and still is the Marches of Brittany, of which it has always played the role of authentic capital city.

The market in Fougères, every Saturday in the centre of town.

▽ ***Painting by Emmanuel de La Villéon: Hay making in the fields of the Salvar park.***
Musée de Fougères Collection.

Useful information

For more information,
please contact :
MAISON DU TOURISME

Office du tourisme
Tel. 99 94 12 20

Pays d'accueil touristique de Fougères,
1, place Aristide-Briand,
35300 Fougères,
tel. 99 99 75 75,
fax 99 99 42 41

Castle:
10 to 12 / 2 to 5
Special hours in summer:
9 am to 7 pm
tel. 99 99 79 59

Saint-Léonard Steeple :
open to the public
Town's Heritage Department

Emmanuel-de-La-Villéon Museum :
open to the public
tel. 99 94 88 60

Camping in Fougères
Paron Municipal Campground
tel. 99 99 40 81
Campsite -
groups
Chênedet-Landéan Farm,
tel. 99 97 35 46

The forest of Fougères
1600 hectares
of woods
and a leisure centre.
Megaliths (the Druids' cord...),
memories of the Chouans...,
walks, horse riding,
mountain biking,
Chênedet lake.

LEISURE AROUND FOUGERES
Chênedet (mountain bike hire,
horse riding,
canoeing, swimming)
tel. 99 97 35 46

Couesnon Valley
(mountain bike hire)
tel. 99 39 34 72

Chauvigné
(mountain bike hire, canoeing)
tel. 99 95 05 64

Montaubert (horse riding)
tel. 99 99 03 52

Villecartier miniature harbour
tel. 99 98 37 24

Mézières (climbing, canoeing)
tel. 99 39 34 72

Dompierre du Chemin (climbing)
Monthault (climbing)

Front cover:
view of the town wall, on the south side; with the castle towers in the background.

Inset:
The fairy Mélusine, patron of the Lusignans... adopted by Fougères! (detail of a stained glass of Saint-Sulpice's church, late 19th century).

Back cover:
Place du Marchix and its old wood panelled houses (16th century), recently restored.

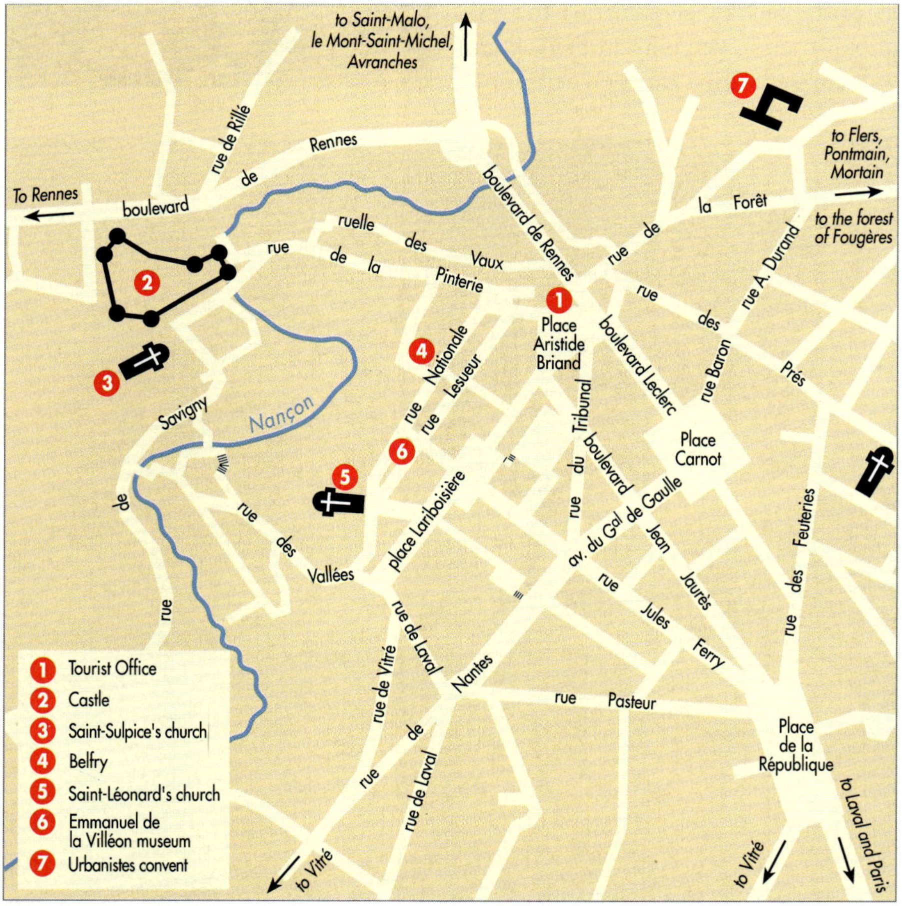

Cartography: Philippe Rekacewicz.

I.S.B.N. : 2.7373.2042.9 - Dépôt légal : février 1996 - N° d'éditeur : 3430.01.03.02.96
Technic Plus Impression, Betton (35)